Creeking and Other
EXTREME KAYAKING

by Elliott Smith

Consultant Daniel Lee
American Canoe Association 1-2 Certified
Outdoor Emergency Care

CAPSTONE PRESS
a capstone imprint

Edge Books are published by Capstone Press
1710 Roe Crest Drive
North Mankato, Minnesota 56003
www.capstonepub.com

Library of Congress Cataloging-in-Publication Data is
available on the Library of Congress website.
ISBN 978-1-5435-7323-7 (hardcover)
ISBN 978-1-5435-7329-9 (ebook pdf)

Editorial Credits
Anna Butzer, editor; Cynthia Della-Rovere, designer;
Kelly Garvin, media researcher; Katy LaVigne, production specialist

Photo Credits
Alamy: Design Pics Inc/Joe Stock, 14-15, Tim Harvey, 17; Capstone Press/Karon Dubke, 12 (bottom); Newscom:
Larry Clouse/Cal Sport Media, 27, Michael DeYoung Blend Images, 29; Photo courtesy of kayaker, Tyler Bradt/
photographer, Lane Jacobs, 5; Shutterstock: Ammit Jack, 11, Clinton K, 8-9, Eder, 7, Getmilitaryphotos, 13,
20-21, Gustavo Miguel Fernandes, 18, Monkey Business Images, cover, back cover, Petr Toman, 25, pp1, 22-23,
terekhov igor, 12 (top)
Design elements: Shutterstock: pupsy, sasaperic

All internet sites appearing in back matter were available and accurate when this book was sent to press.

Printed and bound in the USA.
PA70

Table of Contents

CHAPTER 1

Over the Top at Palouse Falls

On April 21, 2009, kayaking pro and extreme athlete Tyler Bradt could hardly contain his excitement. After many years of preparation and training, he was ready for his biggest challenge. With the sound of the rushing water filling his ears, Bradt began to paddle his kayak to the edge of the Palouse Falls in Washington. He steered the kayak to the drop point, and in an instant, he was falling!

"You're excited, and you're a little scared," Bradt said. "It takes full focus and full commitment. You experience the full roller coaster of emotions."

Tyler Bradt's drop on Palouse Falls included about four seconds of free fall.

Bradt dropped 189 feet (58 meters) straight down, landing at the mouth of the falls while remaining in his kayak. The paddle he was using split in two during the impact of his landing, but he didn't even care. He had done it! He had set a new world record for the longest **descent** over a waterfall. Bradt became a star in the sport of extreme kayaking and creeking that day. His bravery has inspired many athletes to attempt similar drops.

descend—to move from a higher place to a lower place

Creeking?

Creeking is an extreme sport where athletes in special kayaks travel down bodies of fast-moving **whitewater**. It's wet, wild, and no two runs are ever the same. The natural characteristics of a creek help play a role in how the water flows. Creeks or rivers with few rocks feature smoother runs and waterfalls. In rockier creeks, rapids form, leading to drops and swirling water.

The unique boats help the paddler stay safe in the rougher waters and when they face steep drops. Creek boats are designed to be shorter in length. That helps the boat resurface quickly and gives it the ability to bounce off rocks. Creeking is more extreme than regular kayaking due to the water conditions and the hope for big drops.

whitewater—any river or creek itself that has a significant number of rapids

Athletes use quick thinking and cool moves to stay afloat. A key tool is their paddle. They use it to keep the bow of their kayak from going underwater. This move is called **boofing**. It is the most important skill that creekers learn. Athletes using boofing when faced with waterfalls and steep drops. Another important move in creeking is a **jet ferry**.

-a move to keep the bow of the paddler's kayak from
-derwater with a forward stroke at the start of a drop

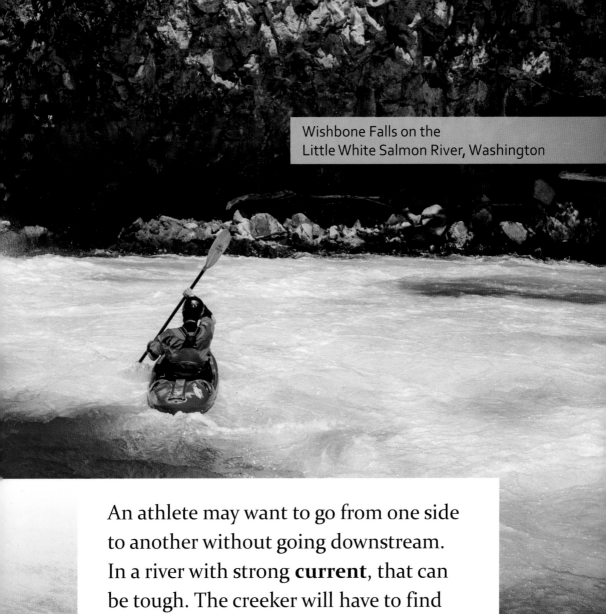

Wishbone Falls on the
Little White Salmon River, Washington

An athlete may want to go from one side to another without going downstream. In a river with strong **current**, that can be tough. The creeker will have to find an area where water is moving upstream. Then, they ride their kayak at an angle to get across safely. The best creekers have some serious skills learned through years of practice.

jet ferry—going from one side of a river to another without moving downstream by riding water flowing upstream
current—the movement of water in a river or an ocean

Many athletes wait until the water is just right before going creeking. If there is too much or too little water, attempting a run can be difficult. A creek or river with more water than usual may hide dangers such as holes. A hole is where the water on top flows upstream but below the surface flows downstream. These spinning features can make it difficult for creekers to escape.

First Descent

Creekers have started to discover ideal waterways around the world. The initial run down a new body of water is called a first descent. To prepare, kayakers do their homework! They look for regions of the world that have good conditions for creeking. Places with coastal mountain ranges usually have the right kind of climate and moisture. Then, they check maps to study the land around the water. Finally, they check the water itself to determine speed, drops, **obstacles**, and exit paths.

With plenty of water yet to be explored, kayakers are always on the hunt for a first descent. New rivers and creeks mean new challenges for these extreme athletes.

obstacle—an object or barrier that competitors must avoid during a race

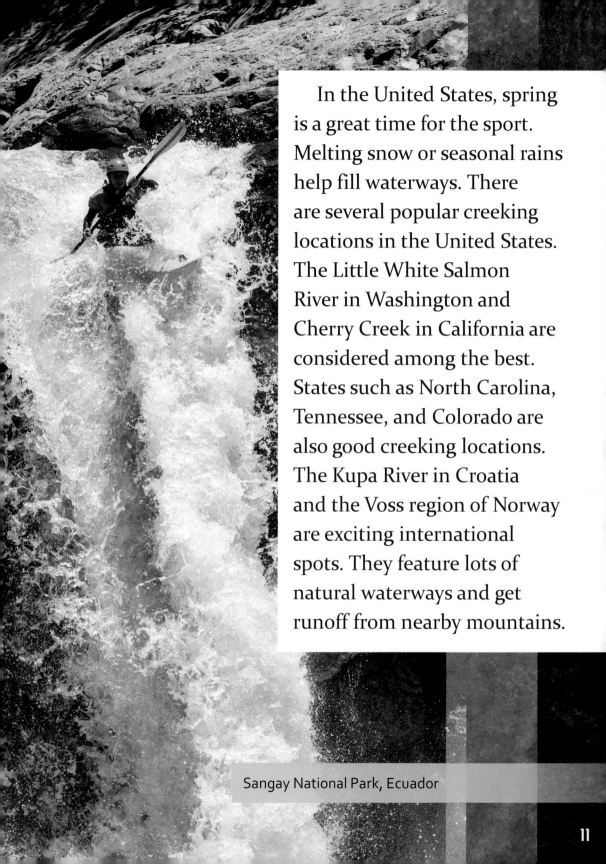

In the United States, spring is a great time for the sport. Melting snow or seasonal rains help fill waterways. There are several popular creeking locations in the United States. The Little White Salmon River in Washington and Cherry Creek in California are considered among the best. States such as North Carolina, Tennessee, and Colorado are also good creeking locations. The Kupa River in Croatia and the Voss region of Norway are exciting international spots. They feature lots of natural waterways and get runoff from nearby mountains.

Sangay National Park, Ecuador

Visual Glossary

paddle
The paddle is critical to success. Athletes must always keep their paddle moving or the boat will spin out of control. They use a short paddle and keep a wide grip.

whistle
If an athlete finds themself in trouble, they can use a whistle to get someone's attention and get help.

kayak
Kayaks range from 5 to 6 feet (1.5 to 1.8 m) in length and weigh 25 to 35 pounds (11 to 16 kg).

RESCUE THROW BAG 50'

throw bag
A throw bag is a bag of floating rope that is thrown across water to help rescue a swimmer.

helmet
A helmet should stay in place and not move around when strapped on. Helmets help keep athletes safe if they hit their heads underwater.

personal flotation device (PFD)
A PFD is required for all paddlers. Even the most experienced athletes need to wear them.

dry suit
Dry suits allow athletes to stay warm and dry while in the water.

spray deck
A spray deck helps keep water out of the kayak.

elbow pads
Elbow pads can protect a paddler's elbows when spending time in rocky areas.

CHAPTER 3

Whitewater Packrafting

Packrafting is a sport that uses an inflatable boat that can be stored in a backpack. It began by combining hiking and rafting. These inflatable boats would be blown up and used after a hike to float on a calm lake. However, packrafting has recently become a more extreme sport. Athletes looking for a little more excitement began taking these bigger boats on faster waters. Packrafts started being used to race down challenging rivers.

Extreme packrafting became popular around the year 2000. Companies began making boats with tougher materials. Athletes modified the boats for higher speeds and rougher waters. Thigh straps are one of the most important changes to the boat. They allow rafters to have more control of the boat. Think of it like tying your shoes tight before playing sports.

Accessories such as spray decks and skirts are also helpful in making packrafts more stable. These **durable** boats have become very popular because they are portable. You can't put a kayak on an airplane, but packrafts can go anywhere—from the icy waters of Alaska to the rapids of the Grand Canyon!

durable—able to withstand wear, pressure, or damage

Surfers around the world stare down huge waves and soar through the air on their boards. Now picture the same thing, except sitting in a boat! Surf kayaking combines two extreme sports into one for maximum fun.

The goal of surf kayaking is to catch ocean waves and surf on them. The athletes use the boat to get to the front of the wave as it breaks. Then they can perform tricks. Traveling along the top of a broken wave is called a floater. A 360-degree turn that leads to a "smack" sound on the wave is a Karate Chop. When kayakers build up speed and jump over a wave, it is called getting air.

World champion surf kayaker
David Speller catches some air.

A surf kayaking athlete catches a wave in Santa Cruz, Portugal.

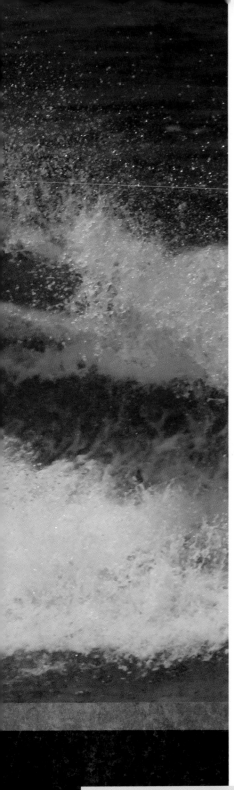

The boats used for surf kayaking are very different from creeking and other kayaking sports. They are made of **fiberglass** instead of plastic. They are curved at the front and flat at the back. This helps the boats go faster. Surf kayaks are about 6 to 7 feet (1.8 to 2.1 m) long and have one or more **fins** underneath. Fins help athletes make quick moves in the water. Turns that put the athlete in the strongest part of the wave are called cutbacks.

Surf kayakers are connected to their boats with braces. These braces keep athletes from falling out when waves crash down around them. They also use their bodies to help with speed. Leaning forward in the boat makes it go faster. Leaning back slows it down. Surf kayakers have to be very good at holding their breath in case they wipe out!

fiberglass—a strong, lightweight material made from thin threads of glass
fin—a small, triangular structure on the bottom of a boat, used to help with steering

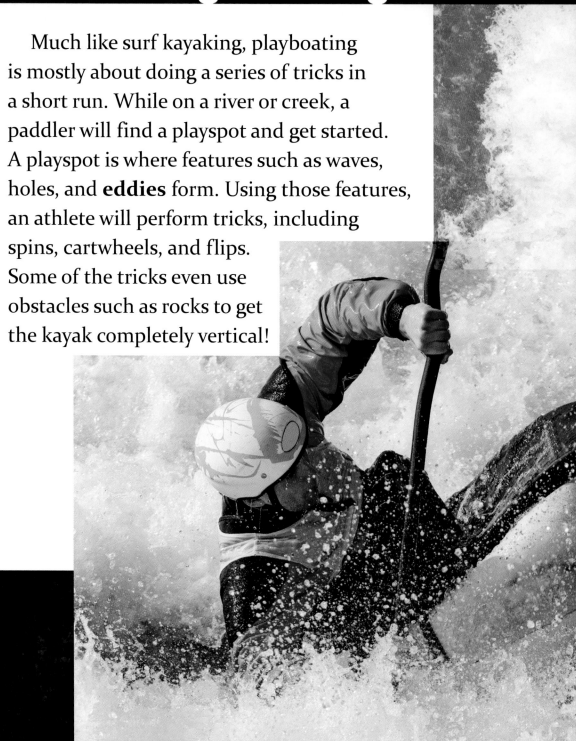

CHAPTER 5

Playboating

Much like surf kayaking, playboating is mostly about doing a series of tricks in a short run. While on a river or creek, a paddler will find a playspot and get started. A playspot is where features such as waves, holes, and **eddies** form. Using those features, an athlete will perform tricks, including spins, cartwheels, and flips. Some of the tricks even use obstacles such as rocks to get the kayak completely vertical!

Being aggressive is the key to success in playboating. Because the playspot is continually active, riders must keep their paddle moving to stay in control of the boat. Playboats are smaller than standard kayaks. This allows athletes to perform tricks more easily.

Athletes don't always have whitewater for working on tricks. And some moves are too dangerous to attempt without practice. So, playboaters often get started by working in flatwater. Flatwater is a calm, level, or slow-flowing water channel. Even in flatwater, athletes get a workout as they use their bodies to power the boats. They also refine their techniques on tricks when they don't have the current to aid them.

eddy—a circular movement of water that causes a small whirlpool

CHAPTER 6

Slalom Kayak and Canoe

Imagine being rushed through rough waters while navigating difficult rapids without going out of bounds. Oh, and you only have two minutes to get through it! That's the challenge of slalom kayak, one of the wildest water sports. Even though courses are man-made, they use the natural features of rivers and streams.

Slalom courses can be set up in natural waterways.

Some of the best race courses are set up on rivers, such as the Payette River in Idaho. Slalom kayakers slide off a 30-foot (9 m) ramp into the water, where a series of eddies and waves await. As the water roars around them, riders must go around a set of gates. These gates play an important role in the race. Officials have set them up as challenges for the racers. They must go through the gates cleanly. Touching a gate is a two-second penalty. Missing one completely is a 50-second penalty. Racers need to use both brains and **brawn** to complete the course.

brawn—physical strength

Racers go upstream and downstream as the current shifts. Athletes must memorize the course and think about the best way to finish it. They need to be strong to **navigate** the rough waters and make quick turns for the gates. Athletes prepare for slalom kayak by practicing on slightly calmer waters. They do need eddies and waves in order to prepare for what is on the course. So, they often go to man-made slalom courses to prepare for the real thing.

Canoe at the Olympics

Canoe and kayak racing became Olympic sports in 1936. But slalom canoe and kayak did not appear until the 1972 Games. The event then went away for 20 years before returning to competition in 1992. Currently, there are four slalom events at the Olympics, three for men and one for women.

Slalom courses at the Olympics are man-made. This is to try and make the race as fair as possible and account for locations without whitewater. Engineers create scale models to test the flow and current before building the Olympic course. Look for slalom canoe at the 2020 Olympics in Tokyo.

An athlete competes in the 2016 Summer Olympic Games in Rio de Janeiro, Brazil.

navigate—to carefully sail or travel over a stretch of water

CHAPTER 7

How to Get Started

While creeking and other extreme kayak sports are fun, it's not as simple as jumping into the nearest stream. Beginners must take steps to make sure they're being smart and safe in the water. Knowing how to swim is very important. All athletes need basic gear, including a properly fitted helmet and personal floatation device. Beginners should always have adult supervision while in or near the water.

Many communities offer programs that teach the basics of paddling and safety, often providing boats and paddles. Those programs may take place at local pools or at nearby lakes or other flatwater locations. The programs can also help you meet other kids who are interested in kayaking.

Tyler Bradt advises new kayakers to find a group of paddlers to learn from. He also suggests just playing around in the water to get comfortable.

Sage Donnelly competes in the women's freestyle kayaking during the GoPro Mountain Games in Vail, Colorado, in 2013.

There are dangers involved with kayaking. Inexperienced paddlers should review the rating of a river before getting in the water. Rivers are ranked on a scale of one to six. Rivers rated as a one are the most calm. Rivers rated as a six have the most extreme rapids. Beginning kayakers should stay within the first two ratings. Beginners should also practice falling out of the boat, swimming to shore, and catching ropes. These skills will help in case anything unexpected happens.

Learning how to kayak can be an amazing experience. Don't worry about going over waterfalls or slaloming down rapids just yet. Even the best extreme athletes need years of practice to get to that point. Beginners should simply enjoy the natural beauty, learn how to participate safely, and have fun.

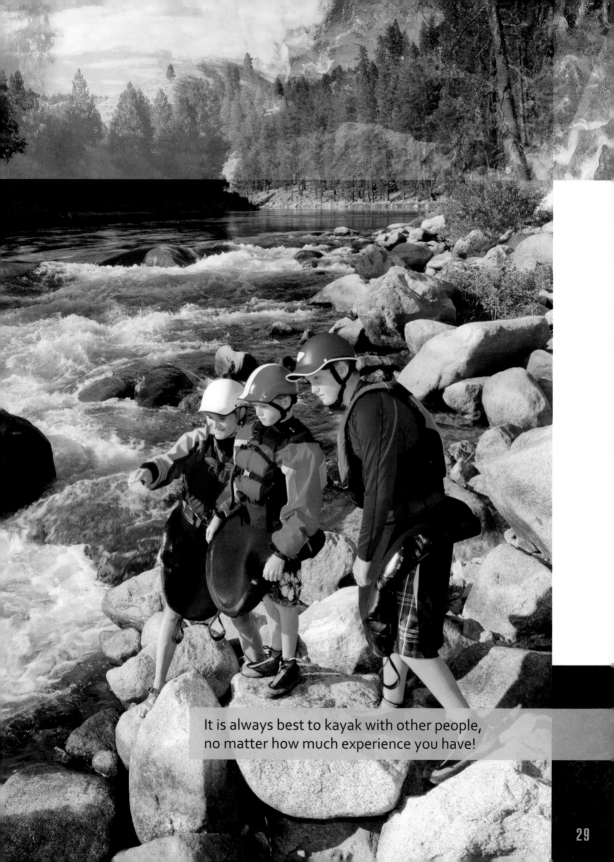

It is always best to kayak with other people, no matter how much experience you have!

Glossary

boofing (BOOF-ing)—a move to keep the bow of the paddler's kayak from diving underwater with a forward stroke at the start of a drop

brawn (BRAWN)—physical strength

current (KUHR-uhnt)—the movement of water in a river or an ocean

descend (dee-SEND)—to move from a higher place to a lower place

durable (DUR-uh-buhl)—able to withstand wear, pressure, or damage

eddy (E-dee)—a circular movement of water that causes a small whirlpool

flatwater (FLAT-wah-tur)—a calm, level, or slow-flowing water channel

fiberglass (FY-buhr-glas)—a strong, lightweight material made from thin threads of glass

fin (FIN)—a small, triangular structure on the bottom of a boat, used to help with steering

jet ferry (JET FAYR-ee)—going from one side of a river to another without moving downstream by riding water flowing upstream

navigate (NAV-uh-gate)—to carefully sail or travel over a stretch of water

obstacle (OB-stuh-kuhl)—an object or barrier that competitors must avoid during a race

spray deck (SPRAY DEK)—a flexible waterproof cover for a boat with holes for the rider's waist

whitewater (WITE-wah-tur)—any river or creek itself that has a significant number of rapids

Read More

Butler, Erin K. *Extreme Water Sports.* Sports to the Extreme. Mankato, MN: Capstone Press, 2017.

Maloney, Brenna. *White Water! T*rue Stories of Extreme Adventures! Washington, D.C.: National Geographic Children's Books, 2017.

Turnbull, Stephanie. *Canoeing and Kayaking.* Adventure Sports. Mankato, MN: Smart Apple Media, 2016.

Internet Sites

American Canoe Org: Youth Page
https://www.americancanoe.org/page/Youth_Development

Canoe & Kayak: Start Paddling
https://www.canoekayak.com/start-paddling/

REI: Kayaking With Kids
https://www.rei.com/learn/expert-advice/kayaking-with-kids.html

INDEX